CW00481085

POCKET BOOK OF
# WISDOM

First published in Great Britain 2019 by Trigger

Trigger is a trading style of Shaw Callaghan Ltd & Shaw Callaghan 23 USA, INC.

The Foundation Centre

Navigation House, 48 Millgate, Newark

Nottinghamshire NG24 4TS UK

www.triggerpublishing.com

Copyright © Trigger Publishing 2019

British Library Cataloguing in Publication Data

A CIP catalogue record for this book is available upon request
from the British Library

ISBN: 978-1-78956-139-5

Trigger Publishing has asserted their right under the Copyright,
Design and Patents Act 1988 to be identified as the author of this work

Cover design and typeset by Fusion Graphic Design Ltd.

Printed and bound in Dubai by Oriental Press

Paper from responsible sources

POCKET BOOK OF

# WISDOM

**TRIGGER**™
The mental health & wellbeing publisher

www.triggerpublishing.com

**the** *Shaw* **mind**
FOUNDATION

Creating hope for children,
adults and families

## INTRODUCTION

Modern life can be filled with so much: from the daily commute, a hectic schedule, cooking an evening meal; to those crucial turning points: quitting your job, moving house, finding love. Between the noise, it can be hard to find those all-important moments of quiet.

The Pocket Book of Wisdom offers a little guidance for when the scales of life are tipped, times become turbulent and a moment of stillness is needed. From the minds of some of the world's most well-known figures, learn to find your footing, take a breath and stand on stable ground once more.

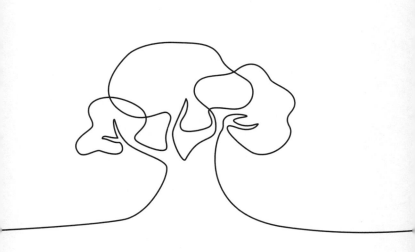

When it is obvious that the goals cannot
be reached, don't adjust the goals,
adjust the action steps

**Confucius**

Yesterday is history,
tomorrow is a mystery,
today is God's gift, that's
why we call it the present

**Anonymous**

I have just three things to teach:
simplicity, patience, compassion.
These three are your greatest treasures

**Lao Tzu**

A tree is known by its fruit; a man by
his deeds. A good deed is never lost;
he who sows courtesy reaps friendship,
and he who plants kindness gathers love

**Saint Basil**

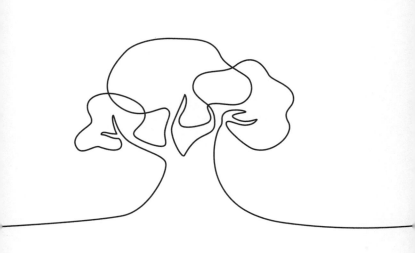

Knowledge comes, but wisdom lingers.
It may not be difficult to store up in the mind
a vast quantity of facts within a
comparatively short time, but the ability to
form judgements requires ...

... the severe discipline of hard work and the tempering heat of experience and maturity

**Calvin Coolidge**

We are what our thoughts have made us; so take care about what you think. Words are secondary. Thoughts live; they travel far

**Swami Vivekananda**

My father said there were two kinds
of people in the world: givers and takers.
The takers may eat better, but the
givers sleep better

**Marlo Thomas**

Wisdom is the right use of knowledge.
To know is not to be wise. Many men know a
great deal, and are all the greater fools for it.
There is no fool so great a fool as ...

... a knowing fool. But to know how to use knowledge is to have wisdom

**Charles Spurgeon**

To know one's self is wisdom, but not to know one's neighbors is genius

**Minna Antrim**

True wisdom comes to each of us when we realize how little we understand about life, ourselves, and the world around us

**Socrates**

Without freedom of thought, there can be no such thing as wisdom – and no such thing as public liberty without freedom of speech

**Benjamin Franklin**

If you're trying to achieve, there will be roadblocks. I've had them; everybody has had them. But obstacles don't have to stop you. If you run into a wall ...

... don't turn around and give up.
Figure out how to climb it, go through it,
or work around it

**Michael Jordan**

A wise man is superior to any insults which can be put upon him, and the best reply to unseemly behavior is patience and moderation

**Moliére**

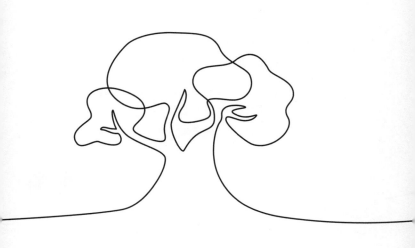

By three methods we may learn wisdom:
First, by reflection, which is noblest;
Second, by imitation, which is easiest;
and third by experience, which is the bitterest

**Confucius**

We should not judge people by their peak of excellence, but by the distance they have traveled from the point where they started

**Henry Ward Beecher**

66

There are many ways of going forward,
but only one way of standing still

**Franklin D. Roosevelt**

Patience is the companion of wisdom

**Saint Augustine**

Never let your head hang down. Never give up and sit down and grieve. Find another way. And don't pray when it rains if you don't pray when the sun shines

**Richard M. Nixon**

The greater danger for most of us lies
not in setting our aim too high and falling
short; but in setting our aim too low,
and achieving our mark

**Michelangelo**

To enjoy good health, to bring true happiness to one's family, to bring peace to all, one must first discipline and control one's own mind. If a man can control his mind ...

... he can find the way to Enlightenment, and all of wisdom and virtue will naturally come to him

**Buddha**

Make it your habit not to be
critical about small things

**Edward Everett Hale**

33

With pride, there are many curses.
With humility, there come many blessings

**Ezra Taft Benson**

In wisdom gathered over time, I have found that every experience is a form of exploration

**Ansel Adams**

Experience is not what happens to you;
it's what you do with what happens to you

**Aldous Huxley**

People don't notice whether it's winter
or summer when they're happy

**Anton Chekhov**

All things must come to the soul
from its roots, from where it is planted

**Saint Teresa of Avita**

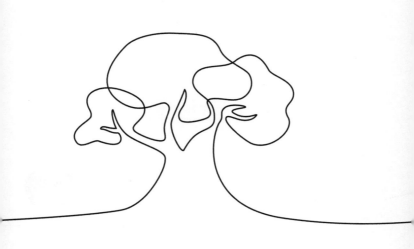

Kindness is more important
than wisdom, and the recognition of this
is the beginning of wisdom

**Theodore Isaac Rubin**

That old law about 'an eye for an eye' leaves everybody blind. The time is always right to do the right thing

**Martin Luther King, Jr**

Never tell people how to do things.
Tell them what to do and they will surprise
you with their ingenuity

**George S. Patton**

To know how to grow old is the master work of wisdom, and one of the most difficult chapters in the great art of living

**Herman Melville**

In dwelling, live close to the ground.
In thinking, keep to the simple. In conflict,
be fair and generous. In governing,
don't try to control ...

... In work, do what you enjoy.
In family life, be completely present

**Lao Tzu**

Don't gain the world and lose your soul;
wisdom is better than silver or gold

**Bob Marley**

Grief can be the garden of compassion.
If you keep your heart open through
everything, your pain can become your
greatest ally in your life's search for
love and wisdom

**Rumi**

And I love that even in the toughest
moments, when we're all sweating it
– when we're worried that the bill won't
pass and it seems like all is lost – Barack
never lets himself get distracted by the
chatter and the noise ...

... Just like his grandmother,
he just keeps getting up and moving
forward ... with patience and wisdom,
and courage and grace

**Michelle Obama**

To make no mistakes is not
in the power of man; but from their errors
and mistakes the wise and good learn
wisdom for the future

**Plutarch**

We learn wisdom from failure much
more than from success. We often
discover what will do, by finding
out what will not do ...

... and probably he who never made a mistake never made a discovery

**Samuel Smiles**

Never interrupt your enemy
when he is making a mistake

**Napoleon Bonaparte**

The only true wisdom is in
knowing you know nothing

**Socrates**

Always keep your mind as bright
and clear as the vast sky, the great ocean,
and the highest peak, empty of all thoughts.
Always keep your body filled with light
and heat. Fill yourself with the power of
wisdom and enlightenment

**Morihei Ueshiba**

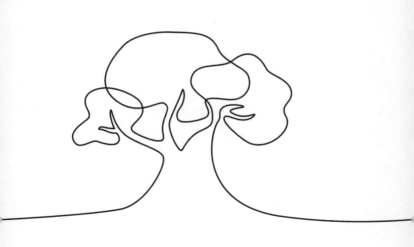

Both old and young alike ought to seek
wisdom: the former in order that,
as age comes over him, he may be young in
good things because of the grace of what
has been, and the latter in order that,
while he is young ...

... he may at the same time be old, because he has no fear of the things which are to come

**Epicurus**

You'll never do a whole lot unless
you're brave enough to try

**Dolly Parton**

Being entirely honest with
oneself is a good exercise

**Sigmund Freud**

Swim upstream.
Go the other way.
Ignore the conventional wisdom

**Sam Walton**

Cynicism masquerades as wisdom,
but it is the furthest thing from it.
Because cynics don't learn anything.
Because cynicism is a self-imposed
blindness: a rejection of the world ...

... because we are afraid it will hurt us or disappoint us. Cynics always say 'no.' But saying 'yes' begins things. Saying 'yes' is how things grow

**Stephen Colbert**

Just as treasures are uncovered from the earth, so virtue appears from good deeds, and wisdom appears from a pure and peaceful mind. To walk safely ...

... through the maze of human life,
one needs the light of wisdom and the
guidance of virtue

**Buddha**

The doorstep to the temple of wisdom is a knowledge of our own ignorance

**Benjamin Franklin**

Never interrupt someone doing
what you said couldn't be done

**Amelia Earhart**

Those who improve with age embrace the power of personal growth and personal achievement and begin to replace youth with wisdom, innocence with ...

... understanding, and lack of purpose
with self-actualization

**Bo Bennett**

Count your age by friends, not years.
Count your life by smiles, not tears

**John Lennon**

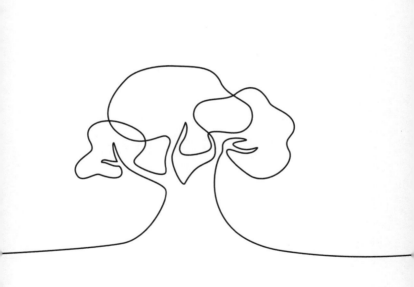

The man who makes everything that leads to
happiness depend upon himself,
and not upon other men, has adopted the
very best plan for living happily ...

... This is the man of moderation, the man of manly character and of wisdom

**Plato**

We humans have lost the
wisdom of genuinely resting and relaxing.
We worry too much ...

... We don't allow our bodies to heal, and we don't allow our minds and hearts to heal

**Thich Nhat Hanh**

I'd rather regret the things I've done than
regret the things I haven't done

**Lucille Ball**

Only put off until tomorrow what you are willing to die having left undone

**Pablo Picasso**

My advice to you is not to inquire
why or whither, but just enjoy your ice cream
while it's on your plate

**Thornton Wilder**

People spend too much time finding other people to blame, too much energy finding excuses for not being what they are capable of being, and not ...

... enough energy putting themselves on the line, growing out of the past, and getting on with their lives

**J. Michael Straczynski**

Leave no stone unturned

**Euripides**

A mistake is simply another
way of doing things

**Katharine Graham**

There is a difference between happiness and wisdom: he that thinks himself the happiest man is really so ...

... but he that thinks himself the wisest
is generally the greatest fool

**Francis Bacon**

Wisdom, compassion, and courage
are the three universally recognized
moral qualities of men

**Confucius**

Everything comes to us that belongs to us
if we create the capacity to receive it

**Rabindranath Tagore**

What would life be if we
had no courage to attempt anything?

**Vincent Van Gogh**

The more you are like yourself,
the less you are like anyone else,
which makes you unique

**Walt Disney**

The philosophy of life is this:
Life is not a struggle, not a tension ...
Life is bliss. It is eternal wisdom,
eternal existence

**Maharishi Mahesh Yogi**

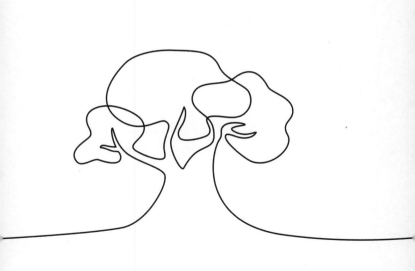

Sometimes I am happy and sometimes not.
I am, after all, a human being, you know.
And I am glad that we are sometimes happy
and sometimes not ...

... You get your wisdom working by having different emotions

**Yoko Ono**

Imagination is more important
than knowledge

**Albert Einstein**

We gain the strength of the
temptation we resist

**Ralph Waldo Emerson**

If you have the guts to keep making mistakes,
your wisdom and intelligence leap forward
with huge momentum

**Holly Near**

Our happiness depends on
wisdom all the way

**Sophocles**

Wisdom begins in wonder

**Socrates**

A good head and a good heart
are always a formidable combination

**Nelson Mandela**

One's philosophy is not best expressed
in words; it is expressed in the choices
one makes ... and the choices we make
are ultimately our responsibility

**Eleanor Roosevelt**

The pessimist complains
about the wind; the optimist
expects it to change ...

... the realist adjusts the sails

**William Arthur Ward**

It's better to be a lion for a day
than a sheep all your life

Elizabeth Kenny

It is better to risk starving to death than surrender. If you give up on your dreams, what's left?

**Jim Carrey**

If you set out to be liked, you would be prepared to compromise on anything at any time, and you would achieve nothing

**Margaret Thatcher**

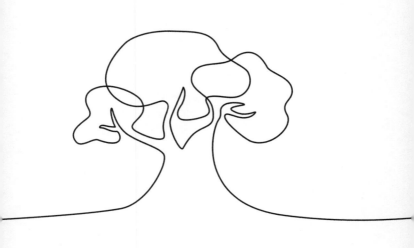

An owl is traditionally a
symbol of wisdom, so we are neither
doves nor hawks but owls ...

... and we are vigilant when others are resting

**Urjit Patel**

Knowledge is knowing that
a tomato is a fruit. Wisdom is knowing
not to put it in a fruit salad

**Brian O'Driscoll**

We all grow up. Hopefully, we get wiser.
Age brings wisdom, and fatherhood
changes one's life completely

**Frank Abagnale**

Look at anyone's bookcase at home,
no matter how modest, and you're
going to find a book that contains wisdom
or ideas or a language that's at
least a thousand years old. And the ideas
that humans have created ...

... a mechanism to time travel, to hurl ideas into the future, it sort of bookends. Books are a time machine

**Jonathan Nolan**

Every man is a damn fool for at least five minutes every day; wisdom consists in not exceeding the limit

**Elbert Hubbard**

It is the neglect of timely repair that
makes rebuilding necessary

**Richard Whately**

None knows the weight of another's burden

**George Herbert**

The more sand that has escaped
from the hourglass of our life, the clearer
we should see through it

**Jean Paul**

Wisdom ceases to be wisdom
when it becomes too proud to weep,
too grave to laugh, and too selfish
to seek other than itself

**Khalil Gibran**

The opportunity for brotherhood
presents itself every time you
meet a human being

**Jane Wyman**

Teach your children poetry; it opens
the mind, lends grace to wisdom and makes
the heroic virtues hereditary

**Walter Scott**

A little knowledge that acts
is worth infinitely more than
much knowledge that is idle

**Khalil Gibran**

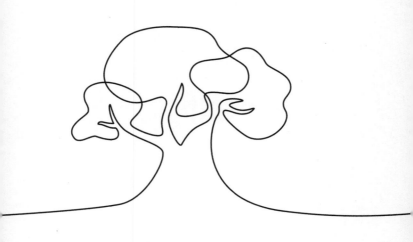

I think it's nice to age gracefully.
OK, you lose the youth, a certain stamina
and dewy glow, but what you gain on the
inside as a human being is wonderful ...

... the wisdom, the acceptance and
the peace of mind. It's a fair exchange

**Cherie Lunghi**

Everything that irritates us about
others can lead us to an
understanding of ourselves

**Carl Jung**

Strength and wisdom are not
opposing values

**William J. Clinton**

Wisdom has never made a bigot,
but learning has

**Josh Billings**

Habit, if not resisted, soon becomes necessity

**Saint Augustine**

Wise men make more
opportunities than they find

**Francis Bacon**

Learning sleeps and snores
in libraries, but wisdom is everywhere,
wide awake, on tiptoe

**Josh Billings**

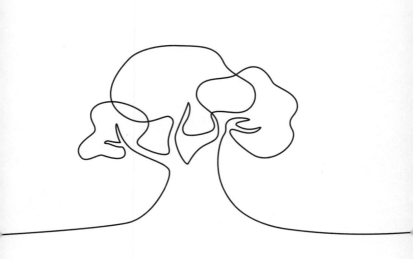

Each of us finds his unique vehicle for
sharing with others his bit of wisdom

**Ram Dass**

To profit from good advice requires
more wisdom than to give it

**Wilson Mizner**

The wheel that squeaks the loudest is
the one that gets the grease

**Josh Billings**

Be as you wish to seem

**Socrates**

139

Do not go where the pay may lead,
go instead where there is no path
and leave a trail

**Ralph Waldo Emerson**

Knowledge without justice ought to be called
cunning rather than wisdom

**Plato**

Don't taunt the alligator until
after you've crossed the creek

**Dan Rather**

Blessed are those who give without
remembering and take without forgetting

**Elizabeth Bibesco**

Back of every mistaken venture and
defeat is the laughter of wisdom, if you listen

**Carl Sandburg**

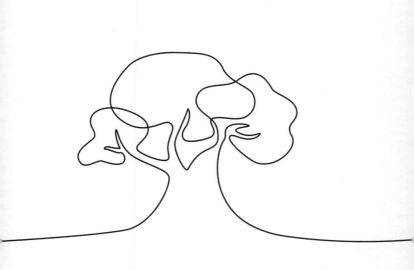

For a little guidance elsewhere ...

POCKET BOOK OF

# COMPASSION

For when life gets a little tough

# POCKET BOOK OF
# RESILIENCE

For when life gets a little tough

POCKET BOOK OF

# BALANCE

For when life gets a little tough

**TRIGGER**™
The mental health & wellbeing publisher

www.triggerpublishing.com

Trigger is a publishing house devoted to opening
conversations about mental health. We tell the stories
of people who have suffered from mental illnesses
and recovered, so that others may learn from them.

**the** *Shaw* **mind**
FOUNDATION

Creating hope for children,
adults and families

**www.shawmindfoundation.org**

We aim to end the suffering and despair caused by
mental health issues. Our goal is to make help
and support available for every single person in
society, from all walks of life. We will never stop
offering hope. These are our promises.